ALL KINDS OF EYES

Sara Swan Miller

Marshall Cavendish

Marshall Cavendish Benchmark
99 White Plains Road
Tarrytown, New York 10591-9001
www.marshallcavendish.us

Editor: Doug Sanders
Publisher: Michelle Bisson
Art Director: Anahid Hamparian
Series Designer: Alex Ferrari

Library of Congress Cataloging-in-Publication Data

Miller, Sara Swan.
  Eyes / by Sara Swan Miller.
      p. cm. — (All kinds of ...)
  Summary: "An exploration of animals eyes, their various shapes and functions"—Provided by publisher.
  Includes bibliographical references (p. 47) and index.
  ISBN-13: 978-0-7614-2519-9
  1. Eye—Juvenile literature. I. Title. II. Series.

  QL949.M64 2007
  591.4'4—dc22

                            2006019713

CONTENTS

The cornea covers the iris,
the colored part of the eye.

1

I SEE YOU

Do you ever think about how important your eyes are? If you have good vision, you probably take your eyes for granted. But think for a minute what life would be like if you had no eyes. You would not be able to play baseball or ride a bike. You would not be able to watch movies or television. If you had no eyes, you couldn't even read this book.

Most people rely on their vision more than on any other sense. People who cannot see, or cannot see well, come to depend on their hearing and sense of touch to get around in the world. But for the rest of us, our eyesight is our most highly developed sense.

How do your eyes work? Your eyeball is shaped like a sphere or globe that has been slightly flattened. The clear dome covering the front of your eye is called the *cornea*. It helps bend the light rays. The light travels through a watery substance known as the *aqueous humor*. Then the light passes through the small opening in the middle of the cornea called the *pupil*. Around the pupil is your *iris*, the part of your eye that gives it color—blue, green, brown, gray, or hazel. When bright light enters your eye,

5

muscles in the iris contract and make the opening of the pupil smaller. In dim light, the pupil *dilates,* or gets bigger, so that more light can enter the eye.

As light moves through your pupil, it passes through the *lens.* Like the lens on a camera, your eye's lens helps you focus images. The lens is able to change shape so that you can focus on near objects or faraway ones. From the lens, the light then passes through a jellylike substance called the *vitreous humor,* which fills the inside of your eyeball. The vitreous humor keeps your eyeball firm so that it does not lose its shape.

Next, the light reaches the *retina* at the back of your eye. This is a thin layer of nerve tissues that sense light. There are special light receptors in the retina called *cones* and *rods.* The cones are sensitive to bright light and allow

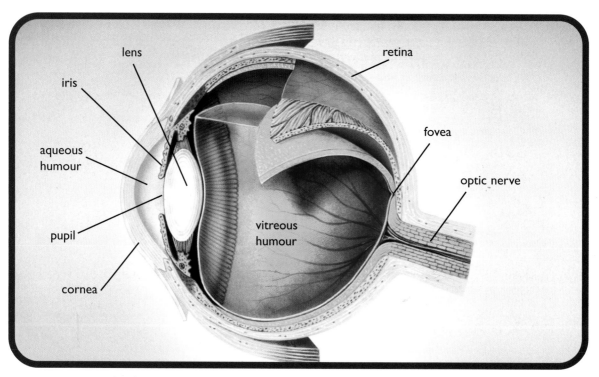

A view of a human eye.

6

us to see color. The rods help us see in dim light, but they cannot pick up different colors. That is why, at dusk, you cannot tell colors apart. Everything looks as though you are watching a black-and-white television.

In the center of the retina is a small, sensitive spot called the *fovea*. The lens focuses the image you are seeing on the fovea. The nerve cells in the fovea are densely packed and help you see details. Near the fovea, the *optic nerve* carries information, in the form of impulses or signals, to the vision centers of your brain. There the brain interprets or reads the impulses as images or pictures. While the process has several steps, it all happens in a fraction of a second.

Other mammals have eyes a lot like ours, but some of these animals see much better than we can. Other creatures cannot see well at all. Whatever the case, the various animal groups have developed the eyes and vision they need to survive. Eyes help animals find mates, locate food, and escape predators. Sight can be a valuable tool in the natural world. Let's take a look at all kinds of animal eyes.

STRANGE SEA STAR EYES

A sea star's eyes are on the ends of its feet! It cannot see actual objects, just light and dark.

A sea star has eyes on its arms.

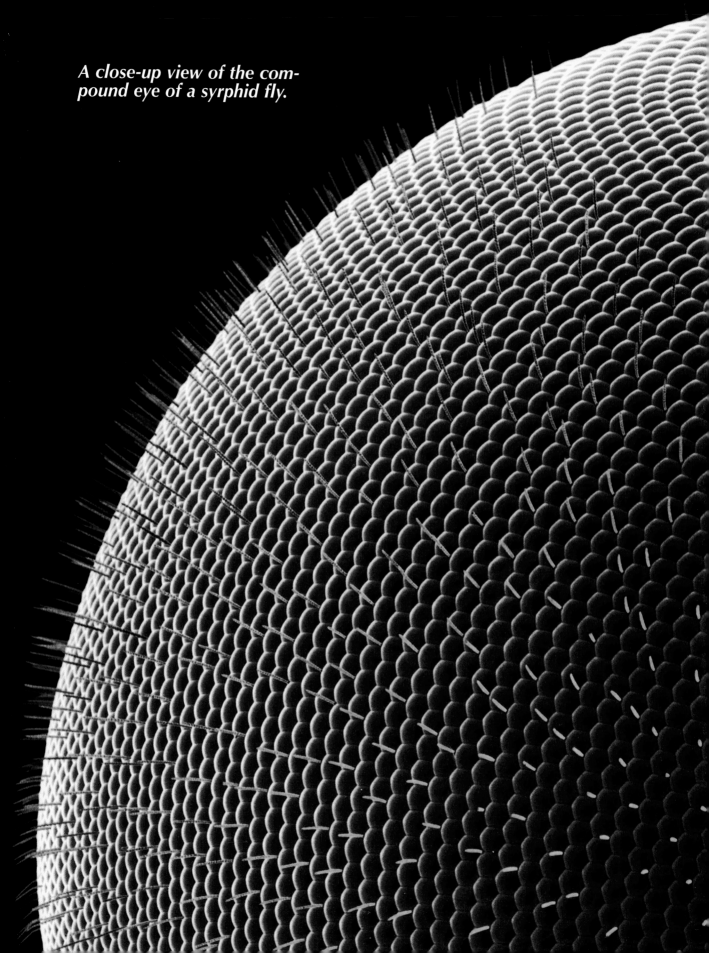

A close-up view of the compound eye of a syrphid fly.

2

INSECT EYES

Most insects have *compound eyes*, and many of them also have simple eyes, called *ocelli*.

Compound eyes are made up of hundreds or thousands of smaller parts called *ommatidia*. Each ommatidium receives an image separately, so what most insects see is a pattern of light and dark dots.

The image an insect sees has far less of the fine detail that we can see. For most insects, the image is fuzzy. Still, compound eyes are excellent at detecting motion. When an insect looks at the world around it, the ommatidia respond to images by turning rapidly on and off. This "flicker effect" allows insects to see moving objects much better than people can. Insects can also see moving objects much better than those that are standing still. If a predator runs or flies into view, an insect will quickly flee. But if the predator is not moving, an insect will not see it at all.

Compound eyes help insects form fuzzy images of the world around them. Most insects also have simple eyes that help them detect light. A fly, for example, has simple eyes as well as two huge compound eyes. Each

EYESPOTS

Other insects trick their predators with big eyespots. A spice-bush butterfly caterpillar has huge fake eyes on its back. An io moth has big eyespots on its underwings, which it flashes open when a hungry bird tries to turn the moth into a meal. A polyphemus moth actually has four large eyespots—one pair on its forewings and another on its hind wings. Big eyespots make a good defense, but you're not fooled, are you?

compound eye has four thousand lenses. Such large eyes give a fly an almost 360-degree field of vision. No wonder it is so hard to swat a fly!

Many insects also have ocelli—simple eyes with a single lens. Insects such as the *true bugs,* which do not go through a larval stage when they are developing, have one to three ocelli on the top of their heads. Caterpillars have several ocelli on the sides of their heads. These simple eyes can detect light, but not images.

Insects can't swivel or roll their eyes the way we can. They really do not need to, though, in order to see what is around them. A praying mantis, for instance, can swivel its head around

A praying mantis turns its head all around, looking for insect prey.

180 degrees. This ability makes it easier for a praying mantis to spot another insect creeping by, then pounce on it and gobble it up.

Other insects have eyes with special adaptations that suit their lifestyle. A whirligig beetle, for instance, spends its days skating across the surface of a pond with its eyes half in and half out of the water. Each of its eyes is divided in two. The top half can focus in the air, and the bottom half can focus underwater. That way, the whirligig beetle can see predators and prey both above it and below it at the same time.

Have you ever seen a click beetle? Did you gasp when you saw those huge eyes on its back? If you looked again, you probably realized that those "eyes" are fake. But birds and other would-be predators are fooled. They think those eyes belong to a much larger animal— one that would be much too big to eat.

DRAGONFLY EYES

A dragonfly is even better at escaping than a fly. Each of its eyes has 10,000 lenses.

A dragonfly's compound eyes wrap around the top of its head.

11

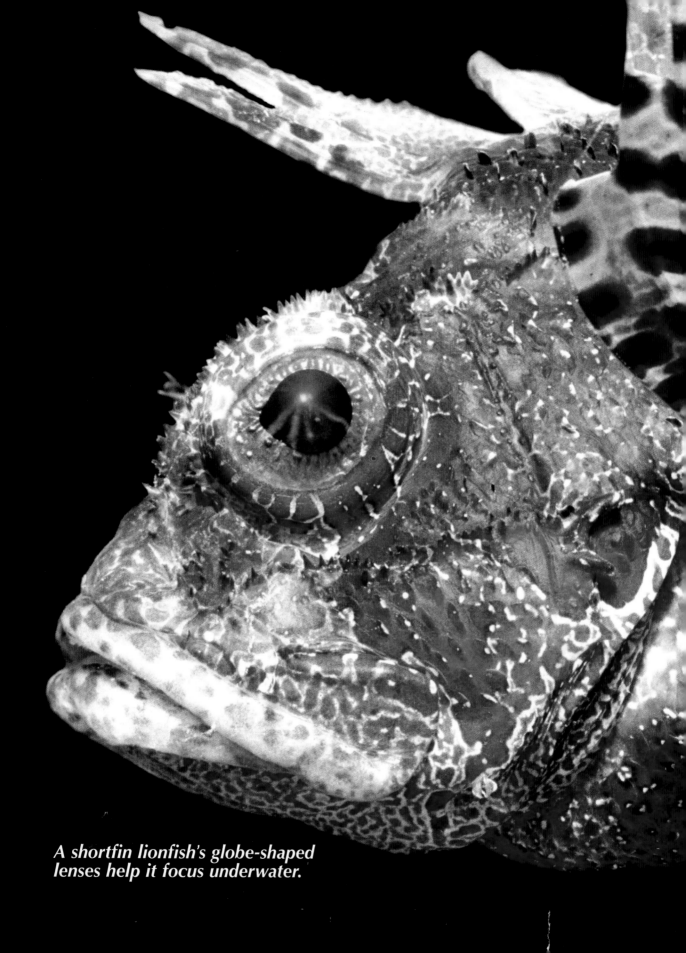
A shortfin lionfish's globe-shaped lenses help it focus underwater.

3

FISHY EYES

Fish eyes are specially suited for seeing underwater. The lenses in our eyes are fairly flat, but fish lenses are globe shaped, which helps them focus better in water. A fish's eye has a cornea, but it is flatter than ours. A fish eye has an iris, too, surrounding a pupil. The iris may be blue, green, black, or bright orange or red. Our pupils can grow smaller or larger to let in more or less light, but most fishes have pupils that can hardly change at all.

Fish eyes are different in other ways. Our eyes focus on close or distant objects by changing the shape of the lens. Fish lenses cannot change shape. Instead, the lens moves toward or away from the retina to focus. Most fishes have eyes on the sides of their heads, instead of on the front as people do. Because of that, a fish cannot focus both of its eyes on the same object at the same time. On the other hand, a fish can spot predators coming from all sides.

How big are a fish's eyes? That depends on

FISH DON'T CRY
Fish don't have tear ducts, and most do not have eyelids. A fish's eyes stay clean and moist because they are always bathed in water.

OLD BRIGHT EYES

If you shine a flashlight at a walleyed pike at night, its eyes will glow in the dark.

where it lives and when it is active. Fishes that live in murky water or that feed at night usually have small eyes. They rely on their senses of smell and hearing to find food. A few deep-sea fishes have large eyes and pupils though. Fishes that are active during the day usually have large eyes as well. But fishes that feed at dawn or dusk, when the light is dim, have the largest eyes of all. Some of these, including the walleyed pike, have a special light-gathering layer of tissue in their eyes.

Some fishes have eyes in distant places. The hammerhead shark has a head shaped like a huge hammer. Its eyes are way out on the ends of its head. This allows it to focus on fast-moving prey more easily.

Other fishes have eyes on the top of their head. The goosefish,

A stargazer buries itself in the sand, watching for a meal to come swimming by

14

the toadfish, and the well-named stargazer lie on the ocean floor, waiting for passing prey. Having eyes on the top of their head means they can spot any prey swimming above. Other fishes that swim or rest on the bottom also have their eyes on top. Manta rays and stingrays, for instance, often swim close to the sea bottom, gazing upward to spot the food they stir up.

A flounder, like other *flatfishes,* has a traveling eye. When it is just hatched, the young flounder has its eyes on opposite sides of its head like most other fishes. But as it grows, one of its eyes starts moving to the other side of its head. By the time it is an adult, both of the

The eyes of this flounder have moved to one side of its head.

15

A BLIND FISH

Not all fish can see. The hagfish, for instance, lives in murky, muddy water where it is hard to see anything. The fish has no actual eyes, just little pits where the eyes would be. However, it can sense light and dark using other areas on its head and tail. But a hagfish doesn't need to see. Mostly, it finds its way by smelling with the single nostril that is found above its mouth.

flounder's eyes are on the same side of its head. The fish lies with its blind side flat on the ocean bottom, watching for food and predators moving above.

Several other fishes have eyes specially adapted to their different habitats and behaviors. The fish known as "four eyes" spends its time at the water's surface. Each eye has a divided retina and pupil. The top part of its eye can focus in the air, while the bottom half can focus underwater. These special eyes help a four eyes watch for predators and food both above and below the water's surface at the same time.

The mudskipper is another fish with specially adapted eyes. It spends a lot of its time on land, skipping through the mud. Being out of the water so much, a mudskipper needs to keep its eyes from drying out. Like other fishes, it has no tear ducts to help keep its eyes moist. Instead, the eyes are covered with a thick layer of clear skin, which protects them from the sand and sun. Every so often, a mudskipper rolls its eyes back into the sockets to keep the eyes moist. A mudskipper can also change the shape of its lenses to see equally well on land or underwater. With its eyes on top of its head, the mudskipper can see both predators and prey passing above. Its vision is so good that it can catch a fast-moving insect as it is flying by.

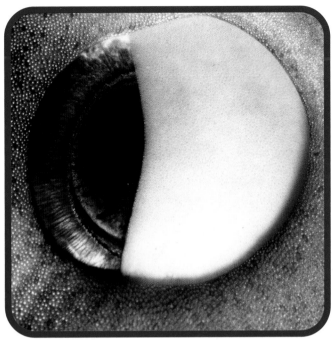

A shark's special eyelid allows it to protect its eyes when hunting and feeding.

Fishes have still other special adaptations. A sea horse can move each of its eyes separately, so it can see in different directions at once. The deep-sea species called the hatchet fish has large bulging eyes that let in a lot of light in the dark waters. A shark has a special way of protecting its eyes. When it seizes its prey, it moves its eyes back into its head. That way, its eyes will not get damaged during the struggle. A shark does not need to see when it is on the attack, because it locates its prey mostly by smell and electrical signals it can sense.

17

Most salamanders cannot see well on land.

AMPHIBIAN AND REPTILE EYES

How well do amphibians see? That depends on which ones you are talking about. Some have sharp eyesight, others see well enough, and still others are nearly blind.

Most salamanders can see, but they usually cannot see well on land. A salamander can normally recognize an

BLIND SALAMANDERS

Some salamanders are blind. The European blind salamander lives in dark underground streams where it is too dim to see. Its eyes never fully develop. Even if it is brought into the light, its eyes won't function. But the blind salamander has learned to thrive in a world without sight. It finds food and gets around using its well-developed sense of smell.

Another blind salamander lives in the mouths of caves as a *larva,* and its eyes work just fine. But when it begins to *metamorphose,* or change into an adult, it travels deep into the dark cave, where it will spend the rest of its life. Then its eyelids draw together until they are nearly fused or joined. The rods and cones of the retina also stop working, until the salamander can no longer see at all. If a larva is kept in the light, though, as it begins to change, its eyes keep developing, and it can see perfectly well.

With its big bulging eyes, a red-eyed tree frog can see all around from its perch.

object that is nearby. But when an object is farther away, a salamander can see only movement or large patches of light and dark. Land salamanders do not really need to see all that far, though. They live in small areas on the forest floor where their insect prey is only inches away.

Salamanders have large pupils but very small irises. In the dark, a salamander's pupils expand or grow to fill the entire eye. Because the eyes let in a lot of light, many salamanders can see their prey even when it is almost totally dark.

Most frogs have strong eyesight. They need to be able to see well in order to snatch an insect flying by. Their big globe-shaped eyes bulging out from either side of their head help them can see all around—from front to side to above and behind all at the same time. This is a benefit to frogs, because there are a lot of hungry predators that enjoy a tasty frog dinner.

Most frogs are *farsighted*—they see objects far away

more clearly than ones that are up close. That makes sense, because a frog that eats flying insects needs to be able to see one zooming in from afar, then leap up to catch it as it gets within range.

THERE IS A LIMIT
A frog is farsighted. Still, it cannot recognize an object that is more than 40 feet (12 meters) away.

The frogs' relatives, the toads, have somewhat weaker vision. If a wriggling worm is more than 10 feet (3 meters) away, a toad cannot see it. But it also cannot focus on prey that is closer than 3 inches (7.5 centimeters). To be able to see its prey clearly, a toad backs up a few inches first, then snatches it with its long, sticky tongue.

Many frogs and toads have beautiful, jewel-like eyes. The iris has metallic gold, silver, or copper patterns over a pastel background. Some frogs have vertical pupils that reach from top to bottom, while others have horizontal ones stretching from side to side. Many frogs feed at night, and their pupils can expand to let in more light. If you shine a flashlight at a frog's eyes at night, they look as though they are all pupil.

Frogs are also sensitive to the differences between light and shadow. If you are walking around a pond, and your shadow falls on a frog, it will leap swiftly away to hide in the deep water. Even though the frog may be looking right at you, it often does not leap away until it sees your shadow blocking out the light.

Unlike fish, all amphibians have eye glands much

More than just for seeing, a frog's eyes help it swallow as well.

like ours. The glands create liquid that flows from the tear ducts and bathes the eyes. An amphibian's tears keep its eyes moist when it is out of the water. Tears also wash away specks of dirt and dust.

Many amphibians can see color. For instance, once a toad has been stung by a bee, it won't try catching a yellow-and-black insect again. Scientists believe that some species of salamanders can see eight separate colors.

An amphibian's eyes are different from ours in some key ways. To focus on an object, our lenses change shape. But an amphibian's lenses cannot do that. Like fish, amphibians have lenses that move closer or farther from the retina to focus. Amphibians' eyelids are different from ours too. Most amphibians have a top eyelid that does not move much and a lower one that does. Usually the lower eyelid is partly transparent or clear. A frog may look as if it is sleeping, but it can still see through its transparent eyelids.

For a frog, eyes are useful for more than seeing. The lower halves of its eyeballs are below the roof of its mouth and actually help the frog swallow. As the frog gulps its prey, it closes its eyes, and the eyeballs press down on its mouth and push the food into its gullet or throat area. A swallowing frog looks as though it is rapidly blinking its eyes.

Reptiles' eyes are similar to the eyes of other land animals. They have a cornea, iris, lens, and retina. But it is in the eyelids where the difference can be seen. While we can move both our upper and lower eyelids, reptiles

EYE WASH

Many geckos have no eyelids. To clean their eyes, they lick them with their tongue.

This tokay gecko is cleaning its eye.

can move only their lower eyelids, which are often scaly. The transparent upper and lower eyelids of many lizards and snakes are actually fused. Their eyes are covered by a large, transparent disk called the *spectacle*.

The spectacles protect a snake's eyes, which do not blink. Over time, though, the spectacles get scratched and dirty. But the snake is not stuck with the same, used pair for its entire life. As it sheds its skin, a snake gets rid of its old spectacles at the same time. Then, for a while, it is able to see quite clearly again.

All turtles rely on their good vision to find their prey, although some can see better than others. Sea turtles, for instance, can see clearly underwater, but when they peer out of the ocean, they are *nearsighted*. Land turtles and tortoises, however, have sharp eyesight when they are out of the water.

Most turtles have large eyes on the front of their heads. Species that live on land keep their eyes focused on the ground when they search for food. Some turtles that live in the water, including snapping turtles and soft-shelled turtles, have eyes nearer the top of their heads. That way, they can hide in shallow water, with only their eyes and nostrils showing. Alligators and crocodiles use the same trick to lie in wait for passing prey.

Have you ever seen a sea turtle cry? Sea turtles have glands near their eyes that create salty tears. The tears help flush out extra salt the turtles take in as they gulp seawater. When a sea turtle is in the water, its tears are immediately washed away. But when a female comes up on land to lay her eggs, her tears keep flowing. It looks as if the turtle is crying from the effort of laying her eggs.

Many reptiles can see in color. Both crocodiles and alligators have rods and cones in their retinas that help them see different colors. Many lizards and snakes attract their mates with their bright colors, and they need good color vision to pick out the right partner.

Reptiles' pupils come in different shapes. Some reptiles have round pupils, some have horizontal

This snake, a boa constrictor, has vertical pupils.

pupils, and some have vertical pupils. For some snakes, vertical pupils are useful. The pupils expand in the dusk, letting in more light, so the snakes can hunt in the dim conditions.

Have you ever watched a chameleon? Its eyes are raised, and it can move each one separately. If a fly zips by, a chameleon can have one eye on its prey while keeping a lookout for predators with the other. When the fly is just in range, the chameleon swivels both its eyes to focus on its prey. With both eyes fixed on its meal, the chameleon can then aim and strike.

The lizard-like tuatara actually has a third eye on top of its head. This eye has a lens and a retina, along with a nerve that connects it to the brain. Scientists are not sure what exactly the third eye does. It may help control the tuatara's body temperature by acting like a thermostat.

Although most reptiles can see well, they detect moving prey much more easily than prey that is standing still. A rabbit might be sitting frozen, unmoving right in front of a snake, but the snake might not even notice it. Sometimes, instead of running off, not moving a muscle is the best way to survive.

This chameleon can move each eye separately or on its own.

These brightly colored budgerigars recognize each other by their colors.

5

A BIRD'S-EYE VIEW

You can probably guess what a bird's most important sense is—its vision! Any bird flying swiftly through the trees needs excellent eyesight to keep from crashing into trunks and branches. Hearing is also important to birds, of course, but their senses of touch, smell, and taste are much less sharp.

A bird's vision is so well developed that its two eyeballs are as heavy as its brain. A bird's eyes are so large that there is no room left in its skull to rotate or move them. The eyeballs are fixed in their sockets by a ring of tiny bones attached to them. You have probably noticed how birds are always swiveling their heads to one side or the other. Since they cannot rotate their eyes, they have to turn their heads instead to get a wider range of vision.

An average bird can see two to three times more sharply than we can. Many birds can also see ultraviolet light, which we can't see at all. Scientists have noticed that some birds, such as budgerigars, have areas of their feathers that look brightly colored when ultraviolet light is shined on them. Budgerigars must look very different to one another than they do to us.

29

A bald eagle has hooded eyes and very sharp vision.

Some falcons use ultraviolet light to hunt for mice. Mice mark their trails with urine, which absorbs or draws in ultraviolet light. To a falcon, a mouse's urine trails look like black lines on the ground. Falcons look for places where there are a lot of trails and keep watch for a mouse to come scurrying along.

Birds that hunt and search for food during the day have retinas densely packed with cones. This helps the bird see well in bright daylight and also to see in color. A bird's eye may have two to five times more cones per square millimeter than ours do.

Birds that hunt at night have few cones in their retinas. Cones are not useful for seeing in dim light. These birds' retinas have a huge number of rods, instead. They aid the birds in seeing in dim light, but they do not pick up color.

Birds with especially sharp vision, such as eagles, have well-developed foveae, the small, sensitive spots in the center of the retina. Some of the high-speed flyers, such as falcons, hummingbirds, and swallows, actually have two foveae. The second one is found to one side of the eye. Scientists think this improves the birds' binocular vision, which helps them steer clear of telephone lines, branches, and anything else that might get in the way of their flight path.

Birds' eyes look a lot like ours. They

GREAT BIG EYES

An eagle's eyes are big when compared to the size of its body. They are almost as large as ours.

EYES OF MANY COLORS

Bird irises come in many colors—black, brown, yellow, orange, white, green, sometimes blue, and even bright red.

have a cornea, a lens, and an iris. Most birds have round pupils like ours, but a skimmer's pupils are vertical slits like a cat's. This bird skims over the ocean surface searching for fish swimming just under the water. In dim light, its cat-like pupils enlarge to a rounder shape. The skimmer can also narrow its pupils to cut down on glare from the water's surface.

You can tell a lot about a bird's habits and behavior by looking at its eyes. Most birds have their eyes on the sides of their head. They have to be constantly on the lookout for danger, and having a wide range of vision helps protect them. They can see what is coming from behind, the side, and in front of them at the same time. To pick out insects, worms, and seeds, they turn their heads to the side.

Raptors, which are hunting birds, have eyes placed on the front of their heads. They need to be able to focus on prey fleeing before them. Binocular vision is good for judging the distance between them and their prey. Birds that hunt in the daytime, such as eagles, also have hooded eyes that cut down on the glare from the sun.

Raptors are known for their powerful eyesight. A wedge-tailed eagle, for instance, can spot a rabbit from the air 1 mile (1.5 kilometers) away. We would need to get much closer—about 550 yards (500 meters) away—to see it at all. A falcon, too, can see a small bird from a mile away.

Like other birds of prey, owls have their eyes on the front of their heads, the better to spot mice running below. Most people think owls are blind in the daylight, but they can actually see perfectly well. At night they can see ten to one hundred times better than we can. Even though its eyes cannot move in their sockets, an owl can see all around it. It has extra bones in its neck, so it can

Like other owls, this gray owl has its eyes on the front of its head.

33

rotate its head up to 270 degrees in either direction. That is almost all the way around.

A woodcock's eyes are different from other birds'. They are set high on its head and so far back that it can focus on things behind it better than objects in front of it. It is hard to sneak up on a woodcock!

Do you know which bird has the largest eyes? The ostrich gets the prize. Its eyes are 2 inches (5 centimeters) across.

Ostriches live in the desert, where fierce sandstorms sometimes rage. Living in such conditions, ostriches developed special adaptations that protect their eyes. They have long eyelashes that keep out the blowing dust and dirt. They also have a *nictitating membrane* over each eye. It is a transparent flap of skin that acts like a second eyelid. It closes

A woodcock has its eyes toward the back of its head.

34

from the inside to the outside of the eye and protects the ostrich's eye while still allowing the bird to see.

Because an ostrich is tall and has such good eyesight, it is usually the first animal to spot danger approaching. When other animals see a fleeing ostrich, they, too, run quickly away.

Even though birds have wonderful vision, there is one exception. The flightless kiwi that lives in New Zealand searches for food at night. Yet it has very poor vision, unlike other birds that are active at night. Being nearly blind is not a problem for the kiwi, though. It finds insects, spiders, and worms by smell. It has nostrils on the tip of its long bill, and it can sniff out insects hiding in the dirt or under the leaves.

BIGGEST EYES

An ostrich's eyes are bigger than the eyes of any other land animal.

An ostrich uses its height and good vision to stay safe.

35

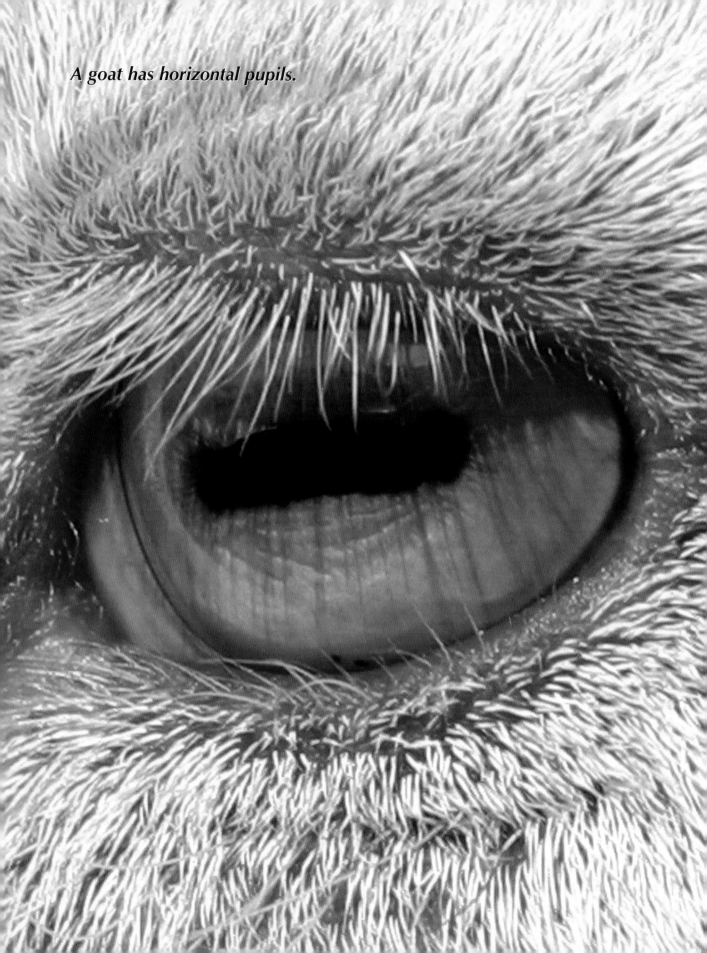

A goat has horizontal pupils.

6

MARVELOUS MAMMAL EYES

Most mammals have eyes a lot like ours, with a cornea, an iris, a pupil, and a retina. But a few have unique pupils. A cat, of course, has vertical pupils that can open wide to let in a lot of light or shrink to cut down on glare. Goats and sheep have horizontal, rectangular pupils set in yellow irises.

You can tell a lot about a mammal's habits just by looking at its eyes. For one thing, you can tell whether it is a predator or a prey animal. Take a look at a wolf, for instance, and you will see that its eyes are on the front of its head. With its eyes facing forward, it can chase after a fleeing animal and keep it in sight. A wolf has binocular vision, so that it can tell just how far away its prey is as it closes in on it. All mammal predators have eyes on the front of their heads, including bears, lions, hyenas, skunks, and meerkats.

All primates also have forward-facing eyes. How else could a monkey see to leap from branch to branch? Mammals that live in trees need to be able to judge distances accurately, and having binocular vision is a big help. Forward-facing eyes also allow a primate to focus on such tasks as grooming and identifying food. Imagine if your eyes were on the sides of your head. How would you focus to read, write, or play tag?

Animals that are preyed on, on the other hand, have eyes on the sides of their heads. They need to be able to see all around to spot predators coming. Many prey mammals have big eyes. Deer, gazelles, rabbits, and zebras all have extra-large eyes that can spot a wolf, a lion, or any other predator creeping toward them even in dim light.

Some mammals' eyes are specially adapted in ways that suit their different habitats and behavior. A beaver, for example, spends a lot of time underwater. When it

When a beaver dives, its transparent eyelids slide across its eyes to protect them.

GIRAFFES ON THE LOOKOUT

A giraffe has huge eyes and very good eyesight. Being so tall, and having such a long neck, it can spot a predator from far away, before shorter, smaller animals would be able to. A giraffe is like a lookout tower for other prey animals nearby. When they see a giraffe fleeing, they also race away from the danger.

dives, transparent or clear eyelids slide across its eyes. The lids act like goggles, protecting the beaver's eyes from dirt and irritating bits floating in the water.

A dolphin's eyes are also well suited to its underwater life. Its eyes are coated with a kind of jelly, which makes the dolphin look as if it is crying. This mucus protects a dolphin's eyes from the irritating seawater. Dolphins' eyes are a lot like fish eyes. The lenses are shaped like globes, which helps them focus well underwater. Dolphins' eyes also have no irises. Instead they have a kind of special lid called an *operculum*. In bright light, the operculum moves down and covers the center of the pupil. That way, there are only narrow slits on the edges of the pupil, and the dolphin can reduce the glare of the sunlight.

Mammals that spend a lot of time near the surface of the water often have eyes on the tops of their heads. A hippo, for instance, spends a lot of time just under the surface, with only its eyes and ears showing. That way, the hippo keeps an eye out for prey and still knows what is going on above the surface.

Mammals that live in the desert have adapted to life amid sandstorms. A camel has bushy eyebrows that help protect its eyes from the blowing sand. It also has a double set of eyelashes that keep out the dirt and grit.

Mammals that are active at night usually have developed a form of night vision. Inside each eye they have a structure called the *tapidum lucidum,* which reflects light and sends it to the retina. These animals can see much

Long eyelashes help protect this camel's eyes from blowing sand.

40

A THIRD EYELID

Some other mammals, including horses and rabbits, also have nictitating membranes, or "third eyelids," on their eyes.

better in dim light than we can. You may have noticed how a cat's eyes seem to glow in the dark. That is the dim light reflecting off the tapidum lucidum.

A cat's eye has yet another adaptation. It has an inner, third eyelid or nictitating membrane, similar to an ostrich's. This membrane slides across the eye and protects it from dryness and damage. Usually, if you see your cat's nictitating membrane, it means the cat is sick. But sometimes a perfectly happy, but drowsy cat will slide its nictitating membrane over its eye.

If you take a closer look at a panda, you will notice that its eyes are a lot smaller than they appear to be at first glance. The large black

A giant panda's eye patches make its eyes look larger than they actually are.

41

patch around each eye makes its eyes look big. Those black patches are actually a special adaptation that protects the panda in two different ways. First of all, the patches help hide the panda's sensitive and fragile eyes. They also help reduce sun glare bouncing off the snow in the high mountains where pandas live.

Most mammals have good eyesight, but not all of them. A manatee, for instance, has small eyes and poor vision. It usually lives in murky water, where objects are often hard to see. A manatee can only see things that are close up. A walrus is another aquatic mammal with tiny eyes and poor eyesight. But since it usually feeds on slow-moving creatures that live near the ocean floor, where the light is dim, it does not need to see well. Both manatees and walruses rely on their senses of smell, hearing, and touch to find food and to move about safely.

Other mammals do not see well, either. A rhinoceros, for instance, has terrible vision. As long as you stand still, the rhinoceros won't be able to see you. But if you move, the rhino will charge without warning. A rhino's eyesight is so bad, though, that it is just as likely to charge into a tree by mistake.

Shrews are active both day and night, but they cannot see well at any time. Their tiny eyes are hidden

BLIND AS AN ANTEATER?

An anteater could not see you even if you were standing just a few feet away.

A walrus's eyes help it spot prey in its icy home.

A pygmy shrew has tiny eyes that do not help it see well.

under their fur. But shrews have excellent hearing and a strong sense of smell. They do not need to see in order to find dead insects or earthworms and grubs.

It probably does not surprise you that mammals that spend their lives underground do not have good vision. A mole, for instance, has tiny weak eyes covered with fur. It cannot see even in the light. It finds its food with its nose instead. A naked mole rat, which spends its whole life in an underground colony, has tiny eyes. Since it can hardly see, it feels its way around with the sensitive hairs on its head and tail.

Do you wish you could see in the dark like a cat? Or spot a little bird from a mile away like an eagle? Thinking about other animals that see better than you do might make you feel a little envious. But then think about how many other animals can only see light and dark, or cannot even see at all. Be grateful for your marvelous mammal eyes!

GLOSSARY

aqueous humor—A watery substance inside the eyeball.

compound eyes—Eyes that are common in many insects and that are made up of many lenses.

cone—A light receptor in the retina that is sensitive to bright light and detects color.

cornea—The transparent cover around the eyeball.

dilate—To expand or grow larger, as a pupil in dim light.

farsighted—Able to see distant objects clearly.

flatfish—One of a group of fishes with flattened bodies and both eyes on one side of the head.

fovea—A small, sensitive spot in the center of the retina.

iris—The area around the pupil that gives the eye color.

larva—The name for the young of some animals.

lens—A transparent structure behind the pupil that focuses light rays.

metamorphose—To develop from a larva into an adult.

nearsighted—Able to see close or nearby objects clearly.

nictitating membrane—A transparent flap of skin in the eyes of some animals that acts like another eyelid.

ocelli—The simple eyes of some insects.

ommatidia—The small parts that make up an insect's compound eye.

operculum—A lid in the eyes of dolphins that covers the pupil in bright light.

optic nerve—The large nerve that carries signals from the retina to the brain.

pupil—The round opening in the front of the eye that lets in light.

retina—A thin layer of nerve cells inside the eyeball that senses light.

rod—A light receptor in the retina that is sensitive in dim light.

spectacle—A transparent disk that covers the eyes of many reptiles.

tapidum lucidum—A structure in the eyes of nocturnal mammals that reflects light and allows them to see in dim light.

true bug—One in an order of insects that have sucking mouthparts and wings that are half thick and half membrane.

vitreous humor—A jelly-like substance inside the eyeball.

FIND OUT MORE

BOOKS

Barre, Michel. *Animal Senses*. Milwaukee, WI: Gareth Stevens, 1998.

Cerfolli, Fulvio. *Adapting to the Environment*. Austin, TX: Raintree Steck-Vaughn, 1999.

Grambo, Rebecca L. *Eyes*. Amazing Animals. Vero Beach, FL: Rourke, 2002.

Hickman, Pamela, and Pat Stephens. *Animal Senses: How Animals See, Hear, Taste, Smell, and Feel*. Buffalo, NY: Kids Can Press, 1998.

Kalman, Bobbie. *How Do Animals Adapt?* New York: Crabtree Publishers, 2000.

Parker, Steve. *Adaptation*. Chicago, IL: Heinemann, 2001.

Santa Fe Writers Group. *Bizarre and Beautiful Eyes*. Santa Fe, NM: John Muir Publications, 1993.

Viegas, Jennifer. *The Eye: Learning How We See*. New York:, 2002.

ORGANIZATIONS AND WEB SITES

The Animal Diversity Web
http://animaldiversity.ummz.umich.edu/
This site contains information about individual species in several different classes of animals, particularly mammals.

Audubon Society
http://www.audubon.org
This organization is an amazing source of information for people interested in birds and bird-watching.

Insect Inspecta World
http://www.insecta-inspecta.com
This site has all kinds of information about insects.

Neuroscience for Kids—Amazing Animal Senses
http://faculty.washington.edu/chudler/amaze.html
At this site you can learn a lot of amazing facts about animal senses.

INDEX

Page numbers for illustrations are in **boldface.**

ABOUT THE AUTHOR

Sara Swan Miller has enjoyed working with children all her life, first as a Montessori nursery school teacher and later as an outdoor environmental educator at the Mohonk Preserve in New Paltz, New York. As director of the school program, she has taught hundreds of children the importance of appreciating the natural world.

She has written more than fifty books, including *Three Stories You Can Read to Your Dog; Three Stories You Can Read to Your Cat; Three More Stories You Can Read to Your Dog; Three More Stories You Can Read to Your Cat; Three Stories You Can Read to Your Teddy Bear; Will You Sting Me? Will You Bite? The Truth About Some Scary-Looking Insects;* and *What's in the Woods? An Outdoor Activity Book.* She has also written many nonfiction books for children.

48